Table of Con

"Tomorrow is the first blank page of a 365 page book. Write a good one."

Brad Paisley

Firsts...

Well, here I am, writing my first ever book! And it all came about after creating my first post on my first ever blog on the first day of 2015. I don't usually make New Year's Resolutions but, back in 2015 I was feeling full of excitement and anticipation for the year ahead and had surprised myself and made a resolution to start a blog. I had also been introduced to "clean eating" but was finding it quite difficult to find a way to incorporate this, in a manageable way, into my busy life as a lone parent juggling work with 3 children. So, I decided to combine the two and began to blog about clean eating with my family, concentrating on keeping things simple but tasty and quick to prepare.

Fast forward 8 years and my life has been (as life often is!) a rollercoaster unfolding in a hundred different ways. My blog has mirrored these changes, the main topic has changed a number of times over the years but I like to think it has remained with an underlying feeling of positivity, love, some funny anecdotes and helpful tips and information to lift, encourage and empathise with all those who are reading it.

I still don't always make a New Year's Resolution but every now and again I do and this year, my resolution was to write a book! I pondered different subjects and then realised that I already had content that people have enjoyed over the years, so why not add to this content and create a series of books, each one concentrating on the different subject areas of my blog!

So, in this episode, keep your eyes peeled for musings about our busy family life along with our clean(ish) eating journey! There are recipes and meal ideas and photos of yummy, clean(ish) and healthy food.

WARNING/DISCLAIMER....I am not a qualified dietician or nutritionist, the recipes in this book may not all be considered 100% clean (hence the "clean(ish)"), but my aim is to get non processed, home cooked healthy meals that are quick and easy to prepare, on the table with a thumbs up from the "little" people around my table and anyone else who joins us! I am real, sometimes I get it right, sometimes I get it wrong, I am new at this 'book writing' business and I'm not even sure I know how to publish this yet so that you can all see it so please bear with me as I start out as a "beginner author"!

Another reason for writing this book is to encourage myself to get back on the clean eating wagon! A lot has happened in the last few years, including having 2 cancer diagnoses. I won't lie, it's been tough. My body has been through the mill and it's been difficult to be as active as I was previously so I need to start taking more care of myself. I wrote these recipes 8 years ago and I'm looking forward to resurrecting them and being kind to my body!

I'll be back again soon, so please keep an eye out for my next release! Thanks for getting this far if you did!

"Once you discover the irresistible magic of eating clean, you can't help but want to share it with everyone."

ToscoReno

The Name T4four

Just a little bit of information about how I came up with the name T4four which in turn will tell you a little bit about me and mine!.....

Firstly, that's what I do a lot of.... make tea for four (myself and my three children, now all grown up at 27, 21 and 18, but at the time of starting my blog they were 19, 13 and 10)! Two are strapping lads (both born weighing over 11lbs!) and one is a (tall for her age) girl and we LOVE our food! I have always enjoyed making them fresh food from scratch and experimenting with different cuisines.

My children often comment on my cooking and how much they enjoy it and, in fact, when they return from trips away from home, it appears they have missed my cooking more than they have me! My 21 year old has developed his own love of cooking fresh food and makes the most delicious meals, I hope encouraged by the meals I have cooked for him over the years. My eldest has just returned from 3.5 years of working and travelling in Australia. He is home for 3 weeks before heading back and we are all enjoying having him back around our family meal table! I am a family girl at heart and having all my "chicks in the nest" is the best feeling ever!

Secondly, the "more" part.... well, I often make for more than four people and I make more than just tea...there is breakfast, brunch, lunch, supper, snacks, nibbles, dinners, cakes, desserts.... you name it, I make it, or I'll at least have a go!

Finally, 4four is the number 44 which is the age I have gone past, so I am now (and will always be) 44 and more!

So, there you go!

The Basics....

So, what is clean eating? Over the years clean eating has been described as anything from simple, healthy meals and changes to your diet, to sticking to a rigid diet that excludes whole food groups.

In my mind, clean eating, is eating food in its purest, freshest form. It's avoiding processed foods and refined sugars, basically cooking things from scratch with fresh natural ingredients. It's eating more whole foods, fresh fruit and vegetables, grains and pluses and avoiding ready meals or food containing artificial substitutes and preservatives.

To keep it simple, these lists may help:

Eat	Avoid
Fresh fruits	White sugar
Fresh vegetables	White flour
Unsweetened dairy alternatives e.g.: almond milk	Processed foods Chemically enhanced goods
Full fat Greek yoghurt (not Greek style)	Artificial ingredients
Cottage cheese	
Cage-free organic eggs	
Whole grain bread	
Whole wheat pasta	
Whole wheat wraps	
Brown rice	
Fresh cuts of meat	
Homemade salad dressings	

"Drink more water...your skin, your hair, your body and your mind will thank you."

Water, Water and Water

Everyone knows that we need to drink more water and I am aware that it's not always easy to do something that sounds so simple! I try and drink at least two litres a day and here are some tips that help me keep hydrated....

- fill a two litre bottle with water every morning and keep it in an obvious place in the kitchen with a glass next to it and pour all drinks from that
- if working, or out and about, fill water bottles from the same 2 litre bottle or take the whole bottle with you
- keep a nice glass bottle of cold water in the fridge and put it on the table at mealtimes instead of glasses of squash. Put it out for the children when they get home from school also. This has encouraged my children to drink more water too!
- drink a glass of water as soon as you get up and another after breakfast, before and after every meal....it will soon become a habit!

If you need a little flavour in your water, instead of processed squash, try making up herbal/fruit teas and cooling in the fridge and serving with lots of ice. Alternatively, fill a jug with cut up fruit, ice and water and keep in the fridge. Let it steep and you have "fruity" water. It's not as strong and sugary as squash so may take a little time to get used to it, but by the time you do, you won't want to go back to that strong squash with the processed taste to it. You can even get water bottles with a little inner section specifically for putting fruit in. If you fill these with fruit and freeze them, you have a nice cool lunchbox drink too!

Kid Tip: Get the kids one of those bottles with the markers on the side that shows how much you should have drunk by a certain time (or mark one up yourself with a sharpie). This is a great way to encourage sibling rivalry/competition to see who can drink the most water and also encourages them to be time aware/help learn to tell the time.

"Imagine lying on a beach, white sand and crystal blue water as far as the eye can see; all around are tropical butterflies in vibrant colours. Zesty and sweet, it's like sipping on an island fruit salad."

The bottom a box of tea from T2!

Time for Tea

As part of a "clean eating" regime, it is recommended to avoid coffee and tea. I know this can be really hard for some people and, as I will often declare, "It's all about the balance."

Unless I'm going at clean eating full pelt (usually after an indulgent holiday or Christmas!), I try and be really strict with myself during the week and then allow myself to have certain treats (within limits) at the weekends. If I do enjoy the odd coffee or tea at the weekend, I don't add sugar or syrup).

So, some tips for replacing tea and coffee:

- Find a nice teapot/special mug you enjoy drinking out of
- Explore some of the fruit and herbal teas available to find one that you like
- Brew your own fresh mint tea by pouring boiling water over mint leaves/stems and allow to steep for 5 minutes

- If you feel the need to sweeten your herbal teas, try just a little organic honey. This is especially nice with lemon based teas and extremely comforting on a sore throat too!
- Take time out to sit down and enjoy your cuppa even if it's just for 5 minutes with a magazine/paper/this book/your eyes closed!
- If you do indulge in the occasional coffee or tea, try and make sure it's organic (organic is better than decaf) and don't add sugar

Kid Tip: Get the kids involved in trying out different fruit teas. Having a tasting session to see if they can guess what fruit is in the tea. This will encourage them to concentrate on their senses and tasting the real flavours in the tea.

Right, time to enjoy my cuppa! Hope you enjoy yours too! :-)

Breakfast for Dinner!

If I have a little time in the morning, I like to enjoy a cooked breakfast. This one is really simple, filling and a firm favourite in our house!

The picture is all the info you need for this one. It is nice and easy.... lean, grilled bacon, spinach and poached eggs!

On the subject of breakfasts, my children often used to have friends over for dinner. I've always welcomed this and love welcoming them round and filling their tummies with healthy delicious food. When I made the following recipe, it was when two of my children were having friends for dinner. I was trying to think of what I could make for dinner that would still be relatively clean and that they would all enjoy. My own children are used to my attempts to gradually introduce them to different foods and different healthy ways of eating. As such they have a varied diet and have always been pretty good at eating veg and salads. However, I was always aware that their friends may not be! So, I decided to opt for one of my children's favourites and add chips as a treat (carrot chips for me!). It is a slightly "naughty" clean meal as pork/bacon etc should be limited/avoided if you are doing "strict" clean eating, but I did buy fresh and not processed. I was so busy making, dishing up etc that I forgot to take photos but basically, we had a cooked breakfast!

- Grilled lean bacon
- Good quality fresh sausages, organic if possible (grilled)
- Poached egg
- Peas (yes, I know you don't normally have these for breakfast but I always like to have some green on the plate!)

Kid Tip: To make it kid friendly and as a treat I did oven chips (you can slice potatoes and cook in coconut oil in the oven) and offered baked beans!

"You are what you eat, so don't be fast, cheap, easy or fake."

Unknown

Smoked Salmon and Scramble!

Another nice breakfast that could also be eaten for lunch or dinner is smoked salmon and scrambled eggs. It's delicious, nutritious and also quick to prepare!

I don't know about you, but smoked salmon and scrambled eggs always feels like a posh brunch! This time I made scrambled eggs with spinach and smoked salmon (and a little grated goat's cheese added to the scrambled egg so it melted in!). It was so delicious I had to force myself to slow down! Right, on with the next thing on my to-do list for today! Let's get busy!

Homemade Burger Tower

Ok, this is one of my favourites and a great "Friday night meal". Burgers tend to go down well with the kids too and this recipe is versatile enough to change to suit your preferences and the children's! You can use your imagination when making your own burger tower and for the children (or yourself!) you could serve it in wholewheat bun or pitta and sweet potato fries! Yummy!

This is how I made mine....

Burger
Combine minced meat (or vegetarian substitute) of your choice with a beaten egg and (optional) garlic, herbs and spices. Make into a burger/patty shape and cook in the oven, grill or pan.

Salad

Prepare a salad of your choice. To keep it really clean, don't use any salad dressings or dribble a little olive oil/lemon juice/hummus over the salad. I like to add avocado to mine.

Tower

This is where you get to be creative! Mine consisted of a cooked portobello mushroom as a base, the burger, some grated hard goats' cheese, a slice of beef tomato and a poached egg.

Serve on the prepared bed of salad, eat and enjoy!

Marinated Chicken

The children loved this dish too.... I even managed to sneak some chopped spinach in with the salad leaves! And there was enough chicken left to make wholewheat chicken salad wraps for the lunch boxes the following day!

I am a very busy, working, single parent who likes making fresh food from scratch for my children and myself. However, I need to take shortcuts to get everything done and one of the shortcuts I make is that I rarely weigh or measure anything! It's a dash of this, a handful of that.... I often make up recipes as I go along or adjust a recipe idea I have found somewhere! Last night I found a lovely recipe for dinner which I adapted to suit my ingredients and our tastes, so here goes!

Ingredients
- 4-6 chicken breasts
- Olive oil (about 2 tbs)
- Balsamic vinegar (about 3tbs)
- Chopped or minced garlic (1-3 cloves)
- Juice of an orange
- Sprinkle of mixed herbs

Method
- Mix all the ingredients together in a baking dish.
- Slit and add the chicken and marinade for as long as you have got (the longer the better!).
- Put in the oven at 180°C until chicken breasts are cooked through. Turn the chicken regularly and tip out the majority of the liquid towards the end of the cooking time.

To Serve
Serve on a bed of salad of your choice with a poached egg on the top. I drizzled the juices from the pan on the salad as a dressing (you then get the yummy flavours of the orange and balsamic). Enjoy!

Spagbol

Bolognese has always been a favourite in this house but yesterday I was able to make it without the usual complications of having a child with lots of food allergies! DS2 has suffered from many food allergies since he was 18 months old, one of the allergies being tomato. As you can imagine this has made many easy family dinners difficult.... Bolognese, curries, chilli, pizza. However, after an appointment with the consultant it appeared that he is not allergic to tomato anymore (waahhaaayyyy!). This is going to make family mealtimes a lot easier, Bolognese in particular, and will be nice for my son to feel like he is eating the same as everyone else. Over the years I have worked out a method to make him a Bolognese without the tomato but it does involve a lot of faffing, so to find out that I can now make a Bolognese the same for everyone is a wonderful thing!

So, yesterday I made a clean Bolognese in the pan and finished it in the slow cooker while I went about my day. Making a clean Bolognese is pretty easy and a great recipe to start out with when you embark on clean eating. Basically, you make it from scratch using fresh ingredients and you can chuck in whatever vegetables you fancy. This is how I made mine yesterday:

Ingredients
- Mince (any type)
- Vegetables (such as garlic, onions, carrots (grated), peppers)
- Herbs (whatever you have in your cupboard, e.g., oregano, mixed herbs)
- Low sodium stock
- Passata
- Tinned tomatoes (or fresh)

Method
- Brown off the mince (you can use any kind of mince, I used beef)
- Soften the vegetables (I used garlic, onions, carrots (grated) and peppers) in the pan
- Add some herbs (sometimes I add curry powder as well), low sodium beef stock, passata and tinned tomatoes, stir until simmering
- Transfer to a slow cooker (if using this method) and leave to cook on slow all afternoon. If you don't have a slow cooker, you can just leave to simmer, stirring occasionally for around half an

hour. The wonderful thing about the slow cooker is that the meat becomes really tender and the flavours really infuse with each other

You can serve this with wholewheat spaghetti or pasta, or if you're trying to avoid complex carbs and keep it really clean, you could serve it with cauliflower, broccoli and herb rice. All you need to do is grate some cauliflower and broccoli, heat up some coconut (or olive) oil in a pan and stir fry the veg and some herbs in the hot oil for 2-3 minutes! It was really delicious and the herbs added a lovely flavour to it.

Vegetable Tagliatelle

So, I've tried cauliflower rice (which I love!) so I thought I would experiment with an alternative to spaghetti with my clean Bolognese. So, I tried making vegetable tagliatelle from carrots and courgette....

It worked out really well and was very tasty and filling! I used a peeler to make ribbons of carrot and courgette and just popped it in the microwave with a couple of tablespoons of boiling water for about a minute. It made the perfect bed for my Bolognese! I was even able to twirl it round my fork like I would normal spaghetti!

Comforting Chicken

I know I've posted about my slow cooked chicken before but I just wanted to share the convenience and versatility of a wholesome, clean chicken dinner. Sometimes I slow cook the chicken to have as a roast (roast potatoes for the children and roasted celeriac or sweet potatoes for me) and sometimes I do it with mash. This week I did it with mashed potatoes for the children and mashed swede for me. We had a selection of vegetables and I tried out crispy kale for the first time. It was lovely sprinkled on the mashed swede and added a lovely crispy texture. I do think I overcooked it a little so next time I will shorten the cooking time!

The children always enjoy a chicken dinner, it's easy to make and you can change it up by using a different selection of vegetables each time. If your children are reluctant to eat vegetables, encourage them to have a little on their plate and to try them with no pressure. The kale chips are great because they are crispy and don't really taste like vegetables at all!

My children have started giving me marks out of 10 for my dinners and this one got a 9.5 and a 10 from my youngest two! My (then) 18 year old doesn't need to give marks, I know by the way he wolfs it down and goes back for seconds that it's had a thumbs up from him!

Crispy Kale

Kale is packed with anti-inflammatory and anti-oxidant properties. It's remarkably high in fibre and iron; it's also high in vitamins K and D, and a great source of calcium. To add to this already impressive list, it's also high in omega-3 and 6, folic acid and Vitamin B6.

To store kale chips properly, place them in an airtight container after they've cooled down from being baked. Seal the container and keep it at room temperature for a week, where they'll last for up to a week.

Ingredients
- Kale
- Olive oil
- Salt

Method
- Remove the stems, then roughly chop or tear the leaves,
- Wash and spin dry your kale (or use a bag). Ensure the leaves are as dry as possible
- Drizzle with olive oil
- Toss to evenly coat the oil all over the kale
- Pop in the oven until crispy (this will depend on your oven and your kale and amount of olive oil used so check regularly
- Season with salt (it's important to wait until the end before you do this or you will get soggy kale which is not so nice!)

"Mistakes are proof that you are trying."

Minced Lamb Thai Curry

I've tried various "diets" over the years and it's finally dawned on me that to get to and stay at a healthy weight it needs to be a lifestyle change rather than a fast fix or fad. I am a realist too and it's also about getting the balance and finding something that works for you as an individual.

I am aware that nothing is a "one size fits all" and that, clean eating may not be for everyone, but I love it and it's something that I can maintain as a lifestyle and, just as importantly, fit round my family to help keep them healthy too.

The following was a very yummy dinner, so yummy in fact that my 18 year old (at the time) wolfed down the extra that I had made! I thought I had made enough to freeze for another day but he had other ideas!

Ingredients

- Coconut oil (about 1tbs)
- Lamb mince (enough for your family)
- Garlic (at your discretion)
- Vegetables of choice (I used onion, celery, carrot and peppers)
- Curry powder/paste (to taste)
- Tomato puree (a small can or a really good squirt)
- Low sodium stock (1 cube in a cup of boiling water)
- Small tin of coconut milk

Method

- Cook the vegetables and garlic gently in the coconut oil until soft
- Add the mince and curry powder/paste and cook until browned
- Add the tomato puree and stir until mixed through
- Add the stock and some boiling water, stir until mixed through
- Add the coconut milk, stir until mixed through
- Bring to a gentle simmer, stirring occasionally until cooked/reduced

Serve with brown rice or rice noodles

Other Tips

- If you want to keep the carbs to a minimum you could serve this dish on a bed of mashed carrot and swede or fresh raw spinach leaves.
- If you make extra to freeze, make sure the rest of the family know this so they leave some! (I learnt my lesson this time!).

Kid tip: My daughter doesn't like rice so I served hers up with slices of warm wholewheat wraps so it looked like a flower! (I find that children (and adults!) are more likely to try and eat something if it is presented well!

Honey Sesame Chicken

I love Asian food and this was a recipe I pretty much made up as I went along, so I was worried it wouldn't taste as good as I hoped, but we were not disappointed!   I actually served this the first time with mash for the kids and I had mine with leftover veg (from my chicken dish the day before!) and coconut cauliflower rice (see paprika beef recipe). It was so delicious and the honey gave it a lovely sweetness! In their usual fashion my younger two gave me marks out of ten. I got an 8.5 and a 9.5! Not bad!

Ingredients
- Pack of chicken breasts (3-4)
- Chopped vegetables of your choice (e.g. Onion, peppers, mange tout)
- Vegetable oil (a glug)
- Sesame oil (a glug)
- Rice vinegar (a little glug)
- Soy sauce (a couple of glugs)
- Tomato puree (a good squeeze)
- Honey (a good glug)

- Sesame seeds (a good sprinkle at the end)
- Spring onions (sprinkle to serve)

Method
- Dice the chicken and cook over a medium heat in the oils until browned all over
- Add the vegetables and cook for a couple of minutes (if you like your vegetables crunchy then add them nearer the end of cooking)
- Add all the other ingredients (except the sesame seeds) and stir well over a low to medium heat, adding small amounts of water as necessary to make sure the sauce doesn't dry out
- Continue stirring and cooking until the chicken is cooked through and the vegetables are to your liking
- Finish off with a sprinkle of sesame seeds and finely chopped spring onions and serve with your preferred choice of accompaniment. For a really healthy version you could serve with cauliflower rice or brown rice.

Sticky Chinese Chicken

I don't know about you but I have a weakness for sticky, sweet Chinese dishes. I rarely eat Chinese takeaway these days.... Mainly because it's not conducive to clean eating, but also because I feel the Chinese style of cooking lends itself to being eaten immediately, straight out of the wok, so I'm always disappointed by the time my takeaway comes out of its foil container!

Imagine my delight when I tried out this recipe posted by a lovely lady on a clean eating FB group that I used to be part of. I made it one evening and I can honestly say it's the most delicious clean eating recipe I have tried so far! My 19 year old, highly critical son loved it as much as I did and when asked for marks out of 10, he gave me a 9.5!!

I served the children's with brown rice and I had mine with coconut cauliflower rice (stir fry grated cauliflower and pure desiccated coconut in coconut oil for about 2 minutes).

So, here is the recipe....please adapt (as I did) for number of servings and likes and dislikes! I might add pepper next time!

Ingredients

- 4 chicken breasts cut into pieces
- Tapioca or coconut flour
- Chinese herbs and spices (your choice and to taste) (I used garam masala and paprika)
- Garlic
- Coconut oil
- Carrots, thinly sliced
- 4-6 tbsp tomato purée
- 3 tbsp gluten free soy sauce
- 2-4 tbsp of honey
- 2-3 tsp sesame oil
- Pinch of chilli flakes

Method

- Evenly coat the chicken pieces in the flour, herbs and spices
- Melt some coconut oil in a pan and add the garlic and chicken and pan fry until starting to brown
- Add the carrots and continue cooking until the chicken is fully cooked and the carrots are starting to soften
- Mix all the other ingredients together and then add to the chicken in the pan
- Add a sprinkling of sesame seeds, simmer and stir occasionally until fully cooked
- Add more sesame seeds if required, stir through and serve.

Paprika Beef with Cauliflower Rice

(Cooked in a slow cooker)

I had the ingredients in my fridge for this ready and was looking forward to it all week! It was worth the wait, the children loved it and when I asked them for marks out of 10, they gave it 10 and my son said it was "perfect"! Happy children, happy Mummy (and healthy)! It's the first time I have tried cauliflower rice and, not being a lover of cauliflower, I wasn't sure if I would like it. However, it was amazing! I loved how it looked just like rice but didn't taste like cauliflower. It made the perfect base for soaking up the delicious sauce from the paprika beef!

Ingredients
- Coconut oil
- Beef (whatever cut you prefer; I cooked this in a slow cooker so pretty much any cut works)
- Small cut vegetables (onion, celery, carrot, garlic)
- Chunky cut vegetables (peppers, onions, carrot)
- Paprika
- Curry powder
- Tomato puree

- Organic low sodium stock
- Natural full fat yoghurt

Method
- Fry the small cut vegetables in the coconut oil
- Add the beef and fry for a few minutes until browned
- Add some paprika and curry powder and stir in
- Add a large squirt of tomato puree and stir in
- Add the stock and stir in
- Transfer to the slow cooker and then layer the chunky cut vegetables on the top and cook until done
- 10 minutes before you are going to serve, add a couple of tbs of natural yoghurt and stir through until heated

Cauliflower Rice
Grate cauliflower and fry in a pan with some coconut oil and a sprinkle of desiccated coconut for 2-3 minutes.

Other Tips
- I served mine with mash for the children, but equally you could serve with brown rice, mashed carrot and swede or on a bed of raw spinach.
- Experiment with the spices depending on how spicy you like it.
- You could make this with any meat...chicken, pork, lamb.
- Make double the amount and freeze in individual portions for a quick meal another time.

Turkey Tacos

Who likes Mexican? If you asked my brood that question, all of their 6 arms (2 arms each!) would go up, they love it so much!! Fajitas, tacos, chilli. Thursday night always used to be fajita night in our house, but it gets mixed up a bit now!

My eldest asked me last night when we could have tacos again so I decided to make them for tea tonight. I usually use a packet seasoning mix but decided to try creating a clean recipe. It turned out that it was really easy, tastes just as good, if not better, than the packet mixes and I already had all the spices necessary in my cupboard! The kids didn't even notice the difference!

I did mine with cauliflower rice (with cumin and peas), a sprinkle of grated hard goats' cheese and limited myself to just two tacos. I hadn't realised that most shop bought tacos were clean (unless you're avoiding corn which some clean eating advocates do recommend) with only two ingredients in them - cornflour and oil!

Ingredients
- Turkey mince (an average size pack, about 500g)

- Oil (a glug)
- Onion (about 1!)
- Garlic (1 or 2 cloves or the "lazy" type garlic in a tube or jar!)
- Pre mixed Mexican spices or use a mixture of what you have in your cupboard (e.g., cumin, oregano, garlic powder, chilli powder/flakes and onion powder)
- Salt and pepper to season
- Water (as much as needed)

Method
- Dice the onions and cook in the oil for a few minutes until soft
- Add the turkey mince and cook, stirring regularly, until the turkey is no longer pink
- Drain any fat as necessary
- Stir in the garlic and all of the spices including salt and pepper to season
- Add about half a cup of water and turn the heat up until bubbling, then turn the heat down to low and put the lid on the pan
- Cook for 8-10 minutes or until the liquid has reduced. Add more liquid if necessary to ensure turkey is cooked through

Serve in tacos, wholewheat wraps or on baked potatoes with salad and cheese in moderation if you're feeling cheeky!

Slow Cooker Chicken

How do you feel when you wake up to snow?
Excited....childish.... happy.... fed up.... moany...? I have
noticed that snow appears to be a bit like marmite....
people either love it or hate it! I LOVE it! I squeal like a
child when I pull back the curtains and see it covering the
world like a crisp white blanket and immediately rush to
wake my children to tell them to look out of the window!
I know it means getting up earlier in order to de-snow the
car. I know it means getting cold and wet! I know it's a
pain. I know it's horrible to drive in and yucky when it
turns to brown slush.... BUT....you just can't beat the
feeling of seeing freshly deposited snow and then being
the first to leave your footprints in it!

So, on this morning after donning my warm clothes and
wellies, de-snowing the car with a broom (it didn't take
long and was much easier than scraping ice!), taking the
children to school and doing some chores and errands, I
wrapped up warm and headed outside for a lovely brisk
walk in the fresh air! I was out for over an hour and a
half and it was fab. I much prefer exercising out in the
elements to being inside on a treadmill and I enjoyed
every minute and can really feel it in my thigh muscles!

So, that's the "Snow" part of this blog title! As for the
"Slow" part.... well, it has nothing to do with the speed I
was walking! I wanted to share last night's dinner with
you which was another slow cooker special. I had

arranged for a grocery shop to be delivered today so yesterday I wanted to do something that would use up some leftover veg plus I had some chicken in the freezer so I ended up making a very mild chicken curry in the slow cooker.

All I did was part cook some chicken in coconut oil and garlic in a pan then put it in the slow cooker. I then poured over some chicken stock (organic, low sodium) with curry powder, garam masala, cumin, ginger and cinnamon, layered some veg on the top and then left it to cook all afternoon. The chicken was lovely and tender and I served it with brown rice for the children and coconut cauliflower rice (a firm favourite of mine!) for me! There was enough left for me to have for tea the following night which was perfect after my long snow walk!

Simple Spring Chicken

We were fortunate enough to get a last minute deal to Centerparcs with my lovely sister and nieces for the second week of the Easter break one year and we picked the perfect week weatherwise. We even managed to sunbathe outside! It was a very active few days and we managed to eat cleanly most of the time too...just a few sneaky beers! We didn't even have ice-cream! (well, the kids did!). We got lots of exercise cycling our bikes everywhere (including up and down a lot of hills!), badminton, table tennis, walking, swimming and whizzing down the rapids and slides! We had a brilliant time and I started a new job not long after we got back which meant juggling two jobs so I was even more in need of quick and easy dinners! So, the title for this dish came from the simplicity of the dish and the lovely Spring weather we were having at the time! Simple Spring Chicken. It was healthy and wholesome and I added a baked potato for the kids. The chicken was slow cooked (popped it in the slow cooker before I went to work) and I just added a fresh chopped salad with a few grapes and sliced strawberries to mix it up a bit and add a little sweetness!

Fish and Chips

Another family favourite of ours is fish and chips. Here is a delicious and easy healthy version! Smoked cod, mashed sweet potato and crushed garlic peas! It was so filling I saved half of it for my lunch the next day! Another version that I have done which is also delicious is salmon, sweet potato fries and crushed peas!

Ingredients
- Smoked cod fillets
- 1 sweet potato
- Frozen peas

Method
- Wrap the fish loosely in foil and cook in a moderate oven until done (20-30 minutes approx)
- Cook the sweet potato in the microwave or oven until soft, scoop out the flesh and mash with a fork
- Cook the peas and then sauté in a little butter and garlic and then crush with a masher in the pan.
- Serve all three together with a sprinkling of pepper if desired!
  PS. I now stink of garlic!

Roast Dinner and Leftover Omelette

So..I've been quiet for a couple of days after a lovely weekend doing the usual.... feeding and entertaining my children and taking them to work, football and being a "soccer mom", as they say in the US! We also had a lovely evening catching up with special friends that we haven't seen for about 7 years. We had a great time with them, although unfortunately it did lead to a couple of glasses of wine and subsequent slip in the clean eating for an evening! Oops! I did warn you I made mistakes!

On Sunday I did my usual trick of utilising the slow cooker so that the dinner could cook whilst I was standing on the side-lines cheering my son on in his football match. We all love a roast on a Sunday and my slow cooker is large enough to put a whole chicken in, so that's just what I did. A clean eating roast dinner is easy. Just cook your favourite, fresh (organic if possible) joint of meat, add lots of fresh vegetables and replace the roast potatoes with roasted celeriac, sweet potato or parsnips (celeriac is my particular favourite and I often roast carrots too). I sometimes add a little honey towards the end of the cooking time when roasting the vegetables, which is yummy, and the kids love it! I tend to use coconut oil for roasting (more on the benefits of this in another post). I love using the slow cooker on a Sunday....it's always nice to come in from the cold to the smell of a roast dinner cooking and being a lone parent, this is as close as I get to my dinner being cooked for me while I'm out!

Everyone gobbled up their dinner and surprisingly I had some leftovers which I managed to put to good use for Monday night's supper.... Let's call it 'Baked Leftover Omelette'! I just whisked up some eggs with a few herbs, laid the leftovers (chicken, broccoli, mashed carrot and swede) in an oven dish, poured over the egg mixture, sprinkled some grated hard goats cheese on the top and cooked in the oven until it was turning golden and served with salad! Easy peasy! It filled us all up and put the leftovers to good use!

Chicken Stroganoff

I had been extremely busy with 2 jobs, my 3 children and a poorly Dad, when I wrote this post…..

Although I haven't had time to experiment with any new recipes, I have continued to eat clean 80% of the time, but I have mostly been using the recipes that I know and love (and are already on this blog!).

This past week, however, I decided to try a couple of new recipes as we all needed a change and something new to try. I love stroganoff, but don't often buy beef so I decided I would experiment with my own recipe for a chicken stroganoff and the result was a rather tasty dish that got the thumbs up from everyone and a request for seconds!

As usual I don't have accurate amounts for you as I am a creative cook and I tend to chuck in what I fancy here and there and depending on how many of us are home. I also try and make extra in the hope that there is enough for an extra couple of portions for the next day or freezer, but this never seems to happen!

Ingredients

- Chicken, chopped (or another meat)
- mushrooms, sliced
- Peppers, sliced
- Full fat yoghurt
- Garlic

- Paprika
- Mustard
- Coconut oil (or other oil to cook)

Optional ingredients/to serve

- a small amount of wine (option and you could use some clean stock instead)
- brown rice or cauliflower rice
- broccoli or other vegetables

Method
- stir fry the chicken and garlic in coconut oil until the chicken is almost cooked
- Add the peppers and mushrooms and cook for a further few minutes
- Add the remaining ingredients and cook through on a low heat, stirring often
- Serve with rice and vegetables of choice. Devour and enjoy!!

Salmon and Lemon Roasted Veg

I love fish but don't cook it enough. I also love a "one pan" dish! I've had a busy day today doing school runs (along with a very smelly episode with some seashells that had been left in my daughter's coat pocket!!), taking family to the airport, visiting my amazing and inspirational 97 year old Nan and catching up on some studying and washing and more school runs!

One of my children was having tea with a friend (a clean homemade burger, no less....thank you Hayley), the two boys had leftovers from yesterday so I only had to make something for myself. My fridge is low so I needed to come up with something from the odds and ends that I could find. I had some salmon and a selection of leftover vegetables so I conjured up this delicious one pan meal all cooked in a baking tray in the oven. It was so easy and very delicious.

Ingredients

- Any vegetables of your choice that roast well. I used celeriac, sweet potato, onion, peppers and courgette

- Salmon fillets
- Herbs (I used rosemary and oregano)
- Lemon
- Sea Salt
- Coconut oil (or other oil of choice)

Method
- Put the oil in a roasting tray in a hot oven to melt
- Cut the vegetables and salmon into similar sized chunks
- Put the veg and salmon into a bowl and coat with lemon juice, herbs and a little sea salt
- Pour veg and salmon into the roasting tray of hot oil and stir to coat
- Put in the oven and cook until browned and crispy (turning every so often)

Chicken and Sweet Potato Curry

I've had a lovely weekend with my children full of homemade food, football and all the other usual Mum stuff! I fancied trying out a new recipe on Saturday evening and since we all enjoy a curry, I tried out one of my friend's favourites. I altered the recipe slightly so I could finish it in the slow cooker while we went about our activities. It was really delicious with lots of flavour and, after asking for marks out of 10 by my children, I was given 8, 9 and 10! I will definitely be making this one again!

Ingredients
- Pack of chicken (3-4ish breasts or equivalent)
- A glug of oil
- 1 onion diced
- Sweet potatoes (about 2)
- Kale (a handful)
- Veggies of choice (this is a great way to use up leftover veg)
- Mushrooms if you have any
- Garlic (a couple of cloves or a spoonful of easy garlic)
- Curry powder or paste (2 tbs)
- Garam masala (a good sprinkle)
- Chilli powder or flakes (to your liking)
- Seasonings (such as salt and pepper, garlic and onion powder, ground ginger etc)
- Can of coconut milk

- Cup of water
- Fresh parsley or coriander to serve (optional)

Method
- Prepare all the ingredients
- Pop the oil in a pan and add the onion, chicken, sweet potato and veg and cook on a low heat for about 5 minutes, stirring regularly
- Add the garlic and spices and keep stirring for half a minute
- Add the coconut milk and water and bring to the boil
- You can then either turn the heat down and cook on low until the chicken is cooked through and the liquid has reduced and thickened or transfer into a slow cooker to cook for a few hours until done!
- Sprinkle with chopped parsley and coriander if using and serve with brown rice or your chosen accompaniment!

Clean Salad Dressings

One of my lovely customers asked me today about salad dressings and what she could use on her salad instead of mayonnaise. It got me thinking about trying out some salad dressing recipes that are clean. Up to now I have done one of the following if I have had a salad....

1. Eaten my salad "naked", i.e., without dressing. However, I struggle with this and although I love salad, I definitely think it needs a little something to stop it from being too bland!
2. Hummus. I often use hummus as a salad dressing. Make sure you buy the full fat version with natural ingredients with no added preservatives or nasties. Better still, you can make your own!
3. Poached egg. Sometimes I top my salad with a poached egg. If you make sure the yolk is runny and pierce the top as soon as you dish it up, the yolk acts as a yummy salad dressing!
4. I have marinated chicken before in a honey mustard marinade and used the cooked juices to pour over my salad, that was really good!

All these are great, but I have to admit, I miss having a bottle of dressing I can drizzle over my salad that is clean. So, I had a little look on google and Pinterest and found lots of lovely recipes. You can try having a look yourself and see what takes your fancy! I found a coconut and strawberry one that brought back memories of the most amazing signature salad at a restaurant in Clearwater, Florida that contained strawberries and a secret recipe dressing. It was so delicious! It's good to change things up and try new flavours…. even with salad dressing!

Valentines Fruit

For those of you who may want to treat your loved ones and family on Valentine's Day (and I encourage you to consider that every day should be Valentine's Day!), why not keep it simple and serve up a delicious platter of fruit (as shown below). Sometimes the simplest ideas are the best! I would be tempted to have a little dipping pot of dark chocolate too!

Omelettes

I was really busy doing housework this morning...so busy in fact that I forgot to eat breakfast and lunch! Believe me, that doesn't happen very often! When I had finally finished and had a shower, I realised I was starving so I wanted something quick and filling......the answer....an omelette! I will admit that I have to be in the mood for an omelette and today was one of those days. I fancied something savoury rather than sweet and had plenty of eggs so I whipped up a quick omelette filled with ham, spinach and goat's cheese! Delicious and filling....it kept me going until we had dinner (sticky chicken no less!!).

Healthy Takeaway

Most people associate healthy eating with deprivation and the loss of things like takeaways at the weekend. However, with a few tweaks here and there you can still enjoy eating out and takeaways and not forgo your clean eating.

My son loves a curry takeaway, so when it was his birthday last week I asked if he would like to have an Indian takeaway with me while we had a couple of hours peace and quiet without my younger two around. The answer was a cool (as only 19 year olds do!) "Yeah, I'll go for that.". I'm not sure which suggestion he was more pleased about mind you.... the curry or the peace and quiet without his siblings around! My eldest is a smidge over 6ft, broad and with hollow legs so he had the whole shebang!

I ordered chicken shashlik which is cooked in a clay oven on a kebab stick with peppers and onions and delicious spices. It doesn't have a sauce but the way it is cooked and the juices from the cooking make it lovely and moist. It came with a lovely fresh salad and a lemon to squeeze over and I had one papadum instead of bread.

Papadums are usually made from lentil or chickpea flour which fits in with the clean eating philosophy. I thoroughly enjoyed my takeaway and didn't feel deprived at all!

Bancake/Bomlette?!

This is a banana omelette that's the bomb! I love these for breakfast, lunch or supper, as a clean treat that feels naughty but isn't!! They are also great if you feel like pancakes, you can make one big one or a few mini ones! You can even make chocolate ones!

Take a look at the photos of these bancakes....do they look clean or not? What do you reckon? They are in fact 100% clean! If you're trying to lose weight along your clean eating journey, I wouldn't recommend eating them every day, but they are great as a treat whilst still staying on track!

I decided to try adding a small scoop of my protein shake powder (vanilla) to make them more stable and WOW...it really did the job and made it a lot easier to make and, more importantly, flip them! I made a few small ones so that I could make an American style pancake stack and I loaded it with berries and some full fat natural bio yoghurt! They were absolutely out of this world!

Ingredients

- 2 x eggs
- 1 x banana
- 1 x scoop of protein powder (or you could experiment with pure cocoa powder and/or a "clean" flour such as coconut or almond.
- Half a scoop of desiccated coconut (optional)
- Coconut oil

Method

- Put all the ingredients in a blender/mixer and blitz until combined and smooth
- Heat some coconut oil in a pan until hot
- Pour the batter mixture onto the hot pan in 4 equal amounts (each one about the size of a small drinks mat)
- Once the pancakes are done on one side and starting to lift at the edges, flip over and cook the other side.
- Serve with a dollop of full fat yoghurt, a drizzle of pure maple syrup and berries of your choice!
- Try and savour every mouthful (this is the difficult part...I just want to gobble it up as quickly as possible, it's so delicious!)!

Enjoy!

Method (for the Bomlette version)

- Prepare a non-stick omelette pan with some coconut oil and get it nice and hot
- Whisk up the eggs with the banana and add the coconut/cinnamon if using
- Pour the egg mixture into the hot pan and cook as you would a normal omelette, pulling in the sides to let the mixture run to the edge of the pan
- Put berries (if using) on one half of the omelette
- Once the omelette is going brown at the edges and looks almost cooked when you lift it up, fold it in half and cook for a few more seconds until it is done to your liking
- Slide onto a plate and serve with full fat natural yoghurt and a drizzle of maple syrup or organic honey

Enjoy every mouthful and watch out for little people because once they get a taste of your bomlette they will want to eat it all!

"A little of what you fancy does you good!"

No Bake Brekkie Chocolate Bars

Well, we've already had "Breakfast for Dinner" as a topic so why not "Dessert for Breakfast" too! It has to be said that I have a very sweet tooth! I love chocolate, cakes, cookies, desserts.......mmmm.... I'm salivating just thinking about it! I know some people struggle to eat breakfast and some people can only manage very basic "breakfasty" type things at breakfast time. However, I could eat most things for breakfast, especially sweet things and desserts! I attribute this to my very lovely Mum who is a terrific cake and dessert maker and will often whip up a quick Victoria Sponge if she knows we are visiting! When my sister and I were younger she used to have dinner parties with her friends/the neighbours and would offer a choice of about 5 desserts! Ok, I'm probably exaggerating a little, but there were always at least 3 desserts (or puddings as we used to call them!) on the menu. Luckily, for my sister and I, there was always some left and this is where dessert for breakfast came in. We used to love waking up in the morning, after one of my Mum and Dad's dinner parties, to see what leftovers Mum would serve us for breakfast as a special treat!

Where is this leading, I hear you ask?...Well, to keep on track with clean eating and in my quest to lose a few pounds and stay healthy, I like to try out sweet but clean recipes every now and then! So, last week I tried these chocolate bars and they were amazing! I probably didn't make them last quite as long as they should have done but I will definitely be making them again. Next time I am going to keep them in individual portions in the freezer (they do go quite soft at room temperature anyway, so are best kept in the fridge or taken out of the freezer fifteen minutes before you want to eat them - if you can wait that long!) so that I stick to the age old saying "A little of what you fancy does you good"!

Ingredients
- Peanut butter (half a cup)
- Maple syrup, honey or agave syrup (half a cup)
- Coconut oil (quarter cup)
- Vanilla extra (half a tsp)
- Oats (2 cups)
- Cocoa Powder (quarter cup)

Method
- Line an 8-inch pan with baking paper
- Stir together the peanut butter, syrup/honey and coconut oil
- Gently heat these 3 ingredients until the oil has melted and the peanut butter is easy to stir/mix
- Mix in the vanilla extract and then stir in the oats and cocoa powder until everything is well blended
- Freeze until sliceable and enjoy

Tasty Little Bites

Here is another recipe to keep my sweet tooth satisfied! I found this recipe, which I adapted slightly, to make a really lovely alternative to a flapjack. Cut it into little squares and keep in the freezer so that you can just take one or two out about fifteen minutes before you want to eat it. I enjoyed mine with a cup of freshly brewed fruit tea. It was delicious!

This recipe does use a protein powder; however, you can still make these bars without the this, just substitute with coconut flour, almond flour or try experimenting with other "dry" ingredients. This recipe does make quite a lot so you could always halve the recipe.

Ingredients
- 1 cup of protein powder (chocolate or vanilla) or substitute as above
- 1.5 cups of rolled oats

- 1.5 cups of nuts and seeds (your own choice - I added flaked almonds, linseed, chia, pumpkin seeds, coconut etc)
- 1.5 cups of natural, organic, no added sugar nut butter (I used peanut)
- 1.5 cups of honey
- a handful of carob or chocolate (over 70% cocoa) chips

Method
- Heat peanut butter and honey in a pan until almost boiling
- Add dry ingredients and mix well until combined
- Press warm mixture into a suitable baking tray/brownie pan/cake tin
- Push chocolate chips into the top
- Cut gently into squares, chill (or freeze as I do!) and serve when ready
- Eat and enjoy!

Choc-mint Cakes and Reese's Cakes!

These are my own creation and a great sweet treat for when you have a chocolate urge! I love mint chocolate and there is such a small amount of chocolate on these but enough to fulfil that urge! If you're clean eating with the goal of losing some weight (as well as being healthy!) then rice cakes should be reserved for post exercise. These are also a great "after school" snack for the children (if there's any left!). The peanut butter chocolate ones are very yummy too!

Ingredients
- Organic, unsalted rice cakes
- Plain chocolate (over 75% cocoa)
- Organic peanut butter with no added sugar or extras
- Peppermint essence

Method (for Mint Chocolate Cakes)
- Melt chocolate
- Add a few drops of peppermint essence to the chocolate
- Spread a thin layer on each rice cake.

Method (for Reese's Cakes)

- Melt chocolate
- Spread a thin layer of peanut butter on each rice cake
- Drizzle the melted chocolate in lines back and forth over the peanut butter
- Leave until set and keep in an airtight container to enjoy at your leisure! Try not to eat them all at once!

Banana Muffins

Life has been busy and I have had a severe lack of kitchen baking time! This is a shame because I LOVE baking....and I LOVE eating cakes even more! I've managed to get this week of work so I decided it was time to experiment and make something clean for a baked treat and I came up with these yummy banana muffins! This recipe makes 12 muffins. Feel free to experiment with different additions and let me know how you get on. I'd like to try chopped apple in mine next time I make them!

Ingredients
- 3 small bananas, mashed (or 2 large ones)
- 2 eggs
- 2 tbs organic peanut butter
- 2 tbs honey
- handful of raisins (or more depending on preference)
- crushed walnuts/pecans/nuts of choice (optional)
- half a cup of coconut oil, melted
- 1 and a half cups of desiccated coconut/coconut flour

- 1 cup of almond flour

Method
- Preheat oven to 170 C.
- Line a muffin tray with muffin cases.
- Into a bowl place eggs, mashed banana, cinnamon, oil, peanut butter and half a cup of coconut. Mix to combine well.
- Add to the mix almond flour, remaining coconut and honey. Combine well, then stir through raisins and nuts (if using).
- Pour batter into muffin cases (approx. 1 full dessert spoon of mixture per muffin case) and bake for 20-30 minutes or until a skewer comes out clean.

Eat and enjoy!

"What you do speaks so loudly that I cannot hear what you say."

Ralph Waldo Emerson

Clean Packed Lunches

So..this clean eating is starting to rub off on my children! It reminded me of the old saying that goes "Don't do as I do, do as I say!" which is in complete contrast to the saying above! Unfortunately, the former doesn't tend to work with children and, as most of us know, our children are much more likely to copy our actions than they are to listen and do as we tell them! I think it's really important to try and be a good example to our children and live in a way that we would like them to live.

I was amazed one day when my middle son, aged 13 (at the time), came up to me on a Sunday evening and said "Mum, I want to start taking packed lunches to school again and I want them to be healthy. Can we make a salad for school tomorrow?". So, with just a little guidance from me he made this for his lunch! Not only that, but he made one for his younger sister too! I'm not sure which is more of a miracle.... him making a healthy lunch or doing something nice for his sister without being asked!!

Have a browse on Pinterest and Google....you'll find all sorts of great ideas for clean and healthy packed lunches!

Food Swaps

Try these food swaps if you looking at making some healthy food exchanges:

Instead of....	Have...
Pasta	Spaghetti Squash/Spiralised courgette
Mayonnaise	Avocado
French Fries	Baked Sweet Potato Fries
Mashed Potatoes	Cauliflower Mash
Cow's Milk	Unsweetened Almond Milk
Cocoa Powder	Cacao Powder
Fruit Juice	Coconut Water
Vegetable Oil	Avocado Oil, coconut oil, extra virgin olive oil
White sugar	Raw honey, pure maple syrup, coconut sugar
Table salt	Himalayan sea salt
Ice cream	Frozen banana
White rice	Cauliflower rice

One simple change...

That's all it takes to get you on the road to eating clean and feeling healthier, happier, more energetic, clearer skin.... just one simple change a week!

I have come to know the following about clean eating:

- it's a lifestyle change rather than a diet
- I feel so much better when I eat clean
- I am less bloated
- my skin is clearer
- I have more energy
- I lose weight from all the right places (tummy, hips and thighs for me!)
- it saves money
- my children enjoy clean dinners more than "dirty" ones!
- I sleep better
- My mood is better
- the list goes on!

I also know, from being on, and having my own, support forums, that, for some people, going from their old habits to eating clean all in one day/week is just too daunting and overwhelming. This seems to prevent people from trying clean eating as they are worried about failure, sticking to it, eating out, cooking for their families and so on. So, I hope this book serves as an encouragement to you and others to just make one simple change a week to get you and your family used to the clean eating philosophy easily and gradually.

The recipes are designed to be easy and quick to make with ingredients that are easily available.

Enjoy and happy cooking with your family!

I hope you are enjoying this book. It's designed to be one you can dip in and out of and keep to hand in your kitchen for easy recipes at any time. Indeed, the stories attached to the recipes are something that I hope you'll enjoy reading with a cuppa when you have a few moments to yourself.

I'd love it if you could leave a review for this book:

Type the title into Amazon to find it

Scroll down to the "Reviews" section

Click on "Write Customer Review"

They're incredibly helpful both to other readers and to authors.

And lastly, if you enjoyed this, look out for more books in the T4four series including meal planners, journals, notebooks and gifts!

Thank you

Loretta

Printed in Great Britain
by Amazon

43273602R10046